RECRUITING STRATEGIES
FOR THE NEW MILLENNIUM

RECRUITING STRATEGIES FOR THE NEW MILLENNIUM

A Corporate Guide to Building and
Improving Your Company's Recruiting Process

Second Edition

Steve Bullard
*SENIOR RECRUITING
CONSULTANT*

Writers Club Press
New York   Lincoln   Shanghai

Recruiting Strategies for the New Millennium
A Corporate Guide to Building and
Improving Your Company's Recruiting Process

Writers Club Press
an imprint of iUniverse, Inc.

For information address:
iUniverse
2021 Pine Lake Road, Suite 100
Lincoln, NE 68512
www.iuniverse.com

ISBN: 0-595-26362-3

Printed in the United States of America

CONTENTS

INTRODUCTION ix

Chapter 1 *UNDERSTANDING TODAY'S JOB ENVIRONMENT*
. . . . 1
American Workforce Demographics

Chapter 2 *SELLING CAREER OPPORTUNITIES*
. . . . 5
The Sales Model
Applying the Sales Model to Recruiting
An Example of an Effective Recruiting Strategy:
The United States Armed Forces
Discussion of Recruiting Techniques
Finding the Best Candidates

Chapter 3 *IMPLEMENTING THE ACTIVE RECRUITING PROCESS*
. . . . 15
Step 1: Identify Your Company's Personnel Inventory
Step 2: Cost Justification
Step 3: Assigning Resources
Step 4: Creating a Database of Potential Candidates
Step 5: Creating Measurements and Standards
Step 6: You Are Done and Ready to Start Recruiting

Chapter 4   *DAILY OPERATIONS AND FUNCTIONS OF THE ACTIVE RECRUITING PROCESS*

. . . . 25

Using the Internet
Other Sources of Contacts
Get on the Phone
Obtain a Resume
Follow Up

Chapter 5   *THE INTERVIEWING AND HIRING PROCESS*

. . . . 39

The Interviewing Process
Making the Job Offer
Have a Backup Plan
Reviewing the Entire Recruiting, Interviewing, and Hiring Process

Chapter 6   *USING THE ACTIVE RECRUITING PROCESS TO RETAIN EMPLOYEES AND DEVELOP NEW REVENUE STREAMS*

. . . . 47

Salary Information
Marketing Information

REVIEW AND CLOSING 51

ABOUT THE AUTHOR 53

LIST OF TABLES, GRAPHS, FORMS, AND FIGURES

Chapter 1

Figure 1-1: Population Shift by Age Group
. . . . 2

Figure 1-2: Education and Experience of the American Workforce
. . . . 3

Chapter 2
None.

Chapter 3
None.

Chapter 4

Form 4-1: Candidate Information Form
. . . . 32

Form 4-2: Recruiter Call List
. . . . 35

Chapter 5

Form 5-1: Reference Check Form
. . . . 41

Figure 5-2: Recruiting, Interviewing, and Hiring Process
. . . . 45

Chapter 6
None.

INTRODUCTION

The Human Resources manager in today's corporate environment has a tremendous challenge finding, hiring, training, and retaining qualified employees. The key to becoming successful in this arena is to understand the job market and anticipate events before they happen. Getting ahead of the curve will put you ahead of your competition and increase productivity of your workforce. The recruiting process described in this book is proven and used by many of the top recruiting agencies in the country.

If you are a human resources manager or executive in a business and are not satisfied with the success of your present recruiting process, this book is written for you. You will learn a successful approach to recruiting the best employees. Because of the tight job market, traditional recruiting methods are ineffective. Many companies have turned to external recruiters to find qualified employees, which has driven up costs of recruiting. Developing your own successful recruiting process will reduce the costs to your business.

As you read this book, remember that this is a long-term approach that may not produce benefits right away, but it will give you a stable process for future recruiting efforts. Understanding the dynamics of the future workforce will allow you to develop a strategy that works. Following this process will give you invaluable information about the present job market, market salaries, and where to find potential employees.

Chapter 1

UNDERSTANDING TODAY'S JOB ENVIRONMENT

In this chapter, we will examine the American workforce demographics. If you can comprehend the dynamics of the current and future job markets, then you can develop a strategy to take advantage of the opportunities that are available. As with any business challenge, a thorough knowledge of the market is critical.

American Workforce Demographics

Understanding the current and future make-up of the American workforce will help you create a successful strategy. Most everyone has heard about the huge population of "baby boomers" who are growing older and moving into retirement. This fact has created an imbalance in the workforce where there are more older, experienced workers who must be replaced by a smaller, less experienced workforce. Today's companies will need to be prepared to increase productivity through technology and training.

The demographic statistics show that in the year 2000, there are 83,604,000 workers in the age group from 35 years old to 54 years old. In the younger 15 to 34 year old group, there are 81,670,000 workers, which is a difference of 1.93 million workers. This trend is expected to continue for the next eight to ten years. Figure 1-1 is a graph illustrating the population trend from 1990 and projecting to the year 2015.

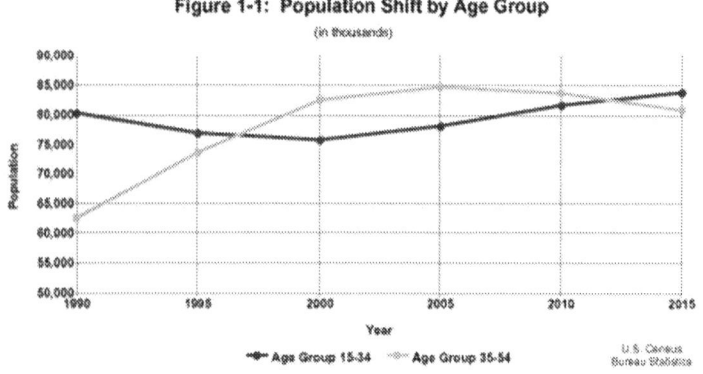

Figure 1-1: Population Shift by Age Group
(in thousands)

Until well after the year 2010, there will continue to be an imbalance in the workforce skewed to older workers. It is critical to understand this fact and understand how it will affect your company. Job positions that require some experience and expertise, such as management, technical, or professional positions, will be harder to fill with qualified employees. Emphasis must be placed on recruiting and training efforts to fill positions left open by retiring employees.

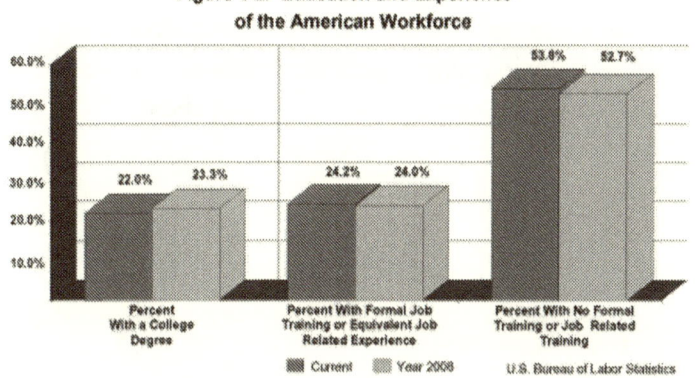

Figure 1-2: Education and Experience of the American Workforce

In addition to the shift in population, there will also be a shift in the education and experience level in the future workforce. Over the next eight to ten years, there will be a greater percentage of the workforce who are college educated, while the percentage of unskilled workers will decrease. While a more educated workforce is desirable, educated workers usually demand a higher salary. This fact is further complicated by the laws of supply and demand. A shortage of qualified workers due to the age shift in the population will naturally drive up salaries. It is already apparent in today's job market where the average employee works for one company for two to three years before changing jobs. Most employees leave because another company makes them a better offer. Gone are the days where an employee works for the same company their entire career. "Job hopping" for a higher salary is very common and will become the norm rather than the exception.

In the near future, labor cost and productivity will become important issues for any business. Understanding the future challenges in the job market will allow managers to anticipate these changes and create a plan to deal with them.

Chapter 2

SELLING CAREER OPPORTUNITIES

What is recruiting? Isn't it really selling career opportunities to prospects? The businesses that are the most effective at selling their jobs, get the best hires. Once you realize this fact and adjust your philosophy to fit the sales paradigm, how you look at your recruiting process will change forever. Selling and sales people have been around since the beginning of mankind and the sales model has been perfected through years of trial and error improvement. Sales techniques that work continue and those that do not are discarded.

Applying the most effective selling techniques to recruiting will give you the most effective recruiting process. Do not try to re-invent the wheel, just use the sales methods that get results.

The Sales Model

Any good salesperson will tell you that the more people that you tell about your product, the more successful you will be at selling. There is an old saying in sales, "the more you show, the more you sell." The key to being a good salesperson is personally networking with as many prospects as possible.

The characteristics of an effective sales process are:
- Building and contacting a long list of prospects.
- Find out the needs of the prospects.
- Tell prospects about how your product or service can fill their needs.
- Build a relationship with the prospect.
- Follow up with prospects on a regular basis and ask for referrals.

Never underestimate the power of word-of-mouth advertisement and personal contact. Building a good relationship with prospects may not sell them on your product, but it may lead to a referral from a friend or colleague of the prospect.

Advertising and marketing play important roles in the sales model, but they should only be used to supplement personal contact, not replace it. There are many drawbacks to relying solely on advertising to sell a product or service. Each prospect has his unique needs and the only way to understand those needs is through a conversation. Advertising puts out a generic message to an audience, but if the message does not resonate with the prospect, he will not be sold on your product or service. The majority of sales opportunities are lost because only advertisement is used to sell a product or service. Advertising should only be used as a tool for name recognition and product information, not selling. The reason why personal contact is so important is the salesperson knows that the prospect has heard his message. With advertisement, there is no guarantee that the prospect will get the message you are trying to convey.

Successful sales people are relentless networkers. They spend their entire day making dozens of outgoing phone calls and personal visits to prospects. Each call or visit is a fact-finding mission to determine the needs of the prospects, how they can fill those needs, and generating referrals from the prospect. These are the same characteristics of the successful recruiter.

Applying the Sales Model to Recruiting

Using the characteristics of the sales model, recruiting should be viewed as building a network of prospects that fit your current and future job openings. Just as a salesperson calls on prospects to sell a product or service, the recruiter should call on prospects to sell a career opportunity. In the recruiting world, prospects are call *candidates*. The more candidates that are personally contacted by the recruiter, the more candidates that will be sold on your business' career opportunities.

Just as a salesperson, a recruiter should be spending most of his day making outgoing phone calls to candidates. Cold calling to complete strangers is difficult for many recruiters, but it is essential to building a network of contacts. The first conversation should be to inform the candidate of the career opportunity and gather information about the candidate. This information will be useful for future recruiting efforts.

There exist a ratio in every sales and recruiting process between the number of contacts made and the number of sales made. Selling and recruiting are a numbers game. Tracking this ratio is essential to managing the process and allocating resources.

The recruiting process described here sounds simple, and it is. Recruiting using a sales approach is not rocket science, it is all about attitude, organization, and competition. Just as a sales-person is competing for customers, recruiters are competing for candidates. A winning attitude with the determination to reach each and every candidate is necessary to compete for those candidates.

An Example of an Effective Recruiting Strategy: The United States Armed Forces

Benchmarking is an effective tool to gathering information about organizations with industry leading business processes. In recruiting, the United States Armed Forces may have the world's most effective recruiting process.

Each year, the Armed Forces must recruit thousands of soldiers, sailors, and airmen to maintain the world's most powerful military force. Talk about a tough sale. How many young men and women would voluntarily give up a job in the private sector to join the military for less pay? Look at the characteristics of the typical military job. Low pay, long hours, difficult working and living conditions, and risk of death. How do they get the recruits to keep the military strong?

First of all, the military deploys an army of recruiters all across the country. The recruiter is one of the most sought after and difficult to acquire positions in the military. The armed forces only select recruiters with a positive image and excellent communication skills. They are the salespeople of the armed forces. These recruiters employ effective selling principles to recruit their candidates.

On any given day, you will see military recruiters at high school and college campuses all across the country. They are making contacts and building relationships with the students on those campuses. By listening to the students, they find out their needs and tell them how a career in the military can fill those needs. They focus on the positives of the military: training, money for college, and patriotism. They do not focus on the negatives: low pay, long hours, or difficult working conditions. Of course, not all of the students buy into the sales pitch, but the recruiters understand that if they talk to enough students, they will find the recruits that they need.

The military spends millions of dollars on advertisement for recruiting, but this only supplements the efforts of the on-the-ground recruiter, not replaces him. Of the new recruits, only a small percentage voluntarily walk into the recruiting office to join. The majority, only join after personal contact with the recruiter.

If the armed forces can sell a military career to thousands of recruits every year, think of the possibilities in your business of employing the same selling principals.

Discussion of Recruiting Techniques

There are two different techniques for recruiting candidates; passive and active recruiting.

Passive Recruiting—This method involves advertising in newspapers, magazines, or job posting on the internet when there is an open position in your business. The distinctive trait of passive recruiting is that the candidate must contact the employer in the form of a resume or job application. An advantage of this method is a lower cost for recruiting personnel. The disadvantages are high advertising costs (newspaper ads are expensive), length of time (it may take a long time to find a qualified candidate), and lost opportunities (you could be missing out on better qualified candidates who are not looking for a job).

Active Recruiting—This method involves pro-actively seeking out potential employees through networking. Active recruiting is a full time, year-round job where the employer is constantly building contacts and following up. The difference from passive recruiting is that the employer does not wait until a job opening is available before looking for a candidate. The advantages of this method are quality candidates (the employer has a choice from a larger candidate pool), quicker response (the employer doesn't have to wait for the candidate to approach him), and negotiating power (the employer will have a greater understanding of the job market and can better negotiate salaries). The disadvantage is the labor and office costs of recruiting personnel.

Hunters and Gatherers:

An analogy to illustrate the differences between passive and active recruiting is the hunters and gatherers comparison.

In prehistoric times, there were two types of people, hunters and gatherers. Hunters aggressively went out seeking prized game using highly honed skills. They traveled across the countryside tracking their quarry and evaluating which animals would best feed their family. One large kill, such as a bison, would feed their family for an entire season. Hunting is a very difficult and time consuming task, but the outcome was worth the hardships. Their endeavors were high effort with high rewards.

On the other hand, gatherers were people that stayed close to home, gathering whatever food was available. They focused on nuts, berries, and plants to feed their families. Gathering took less skill and hardship than hunting, but was sufficient when food was plentiful. Their endeavors were minimum effort for small rewards and their survival skills were limited.

If a hard winter hit, the gatherers would have a more difficult time finding the food necessary to feed their families. On the other hand, the hunters would use their skills to find game even in a difficult environment and their families would survive.

The differences between passive and active recruiting are similar to the differences between hunters and gatherers. When qualified candidates are readily available, it does not take much effort or skill to find them to fill your job openings. Passive recruiting will suffice in a relatively high unemployment environment. As the job market tightens, it becomes more difficult. Just as the hunter must develop specialized skills and aggressively seek its game, the recruiter must develop the active recruiting skills to seek out candidates.

Are you willing to bet the future of your business on the right candidates walking in your door? If so, take the easy, passive approach. If your business is too important to wait for qualified candidates to walk in your door, then create an active recruiting process that will find candidates in any job market.

In today's job market, it may be necessary to do some passive recruiting, but the majority of the recruiting activity should be directed toward active recruiting. In an environment where each qualified candidate may have multiple job offers, the company that most effectively recruits the candidate will have the best chance of hiring him.

An effective recruiting strategy will identify future growth requirements and assess areas of vulnerability. It is important to look at areas of high turnover and determine a recruiting strategy that fills those positions when there is a vacancy. A reality of the job market is that employees will leave a company in pursuit of better opportunities. No business will be immune to this trend, but the business managers that are prepared to deal with this reality will lessen the effect on their businesses. When an employee leaves, productivity is lost while the position is vacant. Reducing the cycle time of finding a replacement candidate means a more productive business and money to the bottom line.

The same theory applies to future growth. The pro-active human resources manager will have a good understanding of the company's corporate strategy and future staffing needs. Business opportunities are lost if a company cannot effectively increase their staff for growth. Businesses that move into new markets or bring a new product to market typically must hire new employees to do so. Quickly finding and hiring these employees may give you the advantage over your competition.

Finding the Best Candidates

As discussed, the most effective strategy to find good, qualified candidates is to implement a sales approach using an active recruiting strategy. This technique requires creating a network of potential candidates. Knowing where these candidates are, understanding their qualifications, knowing their salary requirements, and other vital information gives you the advantage when the need to hire someone arises. There are occasions when time is a crucial factor in the hiring process and therefore having an active recruiting strategy can make or break a company's productivity.

Creating this network of potential candidates is accomplished by making phone calls to these candidates on a regular basis. Asking each candidate for referrals of friends or colleagues will further expand your network. This is a long-term approach and will take months to create. Getting started immediately is important. Implementing the recruiting process outlined in this book will start you down the path to success.

Once a substantial network is created, managing the vast amount of information becomes important. Creating a computer database containing a resume and vital information about each candidate is a good method of managing data, but a simple filing system can be just as effective. The key is that the data must be organized and can be found quickly.

When a need to hire someone arises, finding the candidate becomes quite easy. Simply retrieve all potential candidates from the database matching your requirements and give them a call. If the candidate is not available for hire, ask them if they have a colleague or friend that may fit the open position. This will further expand your network and you will find many new potential candidates.

In the next chapter, a detailed implementation plan is discussed with all of the necessary information to create a successful recruiting process.

Chapter 3

IMPLEMENTING THE ACTIVE RECRUITING PROCESS

Following a logical, step-by-step approach during implementation will ensure success. The implementation process will not be lengthy if the proper steps are followed. This chapter will guide you through the steps necessary to build a world-class recruiting process. The important thing is that you get started. The fruits of your labor will not be fully realized for months and the sooner you start implementing the process, the sooner you will reap the benefits.

Step 1:   Identify Your Company's Personnel Inventory

The first step to implementing any new process is determining your starting point. Once you have identified your company's current situation, you can assess the goals you want to achieve and map a path to get there. In this implementation, it is vital that you look at your current list of employees and ascertain each employee's job requirements. Most companies have a job description for each job, which can be used as a starting point. The key is that you understand each employee's function within the company and their skill-set. The term used to describe this information is the company's *personnel inventory*. For example, if you have two employees that manage the daily operations of your company's computer system, you need to understand their daily job functions, the skills that they use in their job, and technology that they work with. Part of your recruiting strategy should be identifying potential candidates who match your current personnel inventory.

Also part of your preliminary evaluation should be determining areas of risk. These are departments that have a high turnover rate where you must spend a large portion of your recruiting efforts. Evaluate which departments are having excessive turnover and list the positions that have the highest turnover. If there is an area that continues to have high turnover, it may be necessary to assign one or more recruiters to recruiting for that one department. Recruiters that are specialized in recruiting for one area are much more effective because they will become familiar with the skills that are necessary for that department. Understanding these risk areas will allow you to allocate your recruiting resources appropriately.

The final piece of the preliminary evaluation is identifying growth areas. An understanding of your company's long term growth plan will help you to determine which areas you will need to focus resources and the proper time frame for such efforts. It is much more advantageous to be prepared for a large hiring expansion months ahead of time, rather than trying to recruit candidates during the expansion. You must be in contact with department managers on a regular basis to determine their staffing needs for the next few months and the next few years.

Step 2: Cost Justification

Any business that is implementing a new business process, must be able to justify any costs increases. In this recruiting process, there must be personnel assigned to carry out an active recruiting program. You may have the necessary personnel already on staff and you may need to re-structure your recruiting functions to fit the new program. In this case, there will be very little incremental costs associated with personnel. If you do not have the talent necessary to pursue an active recruiting strategy, you will need to hire someone that can carry out the job duties. In a large company that does a lot of hiring, you may need to hire more than one recruiter. As a rule of thumb, if your company is hiring 15 to 25 employees per year, you will need one full time recruiter. If your company is hiring more than 25 employees per year, you will need one recruiter for each 25 new hires.

Other costs associated with active recruiting are internet charges, e-mail costs, internet job posting costs, and computer costs. Most companies already have computers with access to the internet and e-mail, so this may not be an incremental cost.

To justify spending money on your recruiting program, look at the costs that you are spending in your recruiting efforts. External recruiting fees, newspaper advertisements, administrative personnel, and lost productivity. Any manager in your company can probably tell you the money that is lost when there is a vacant position in his or her department. By streamlining the recruiting process, you can decrease the amount of time that a job is vacant and reduce the amount of lost productivity. Below is a simple example of a cost justification analysis.

<u>Cost Justification for Implementing</u>
<u>an Active Recruiting Program</u>

Annual Incremental Program Costs:

Hire and train one recruiter -	$ 65,000
Internet Job Posting Service -	$ 5,000
Telephone/Long Distance -	$ 1,000
<u>Internet Access Fees/E-mail -</u>	<u>$ 600</u>
Total Incremental Costs	$ 71,600/year

Annual Cost Savings:

Newspaper Advertising -	$ 35,000
Administrative Costs* -	$ 25,000
Job Productivity Losses** -	$ 30,000
<u>External Recruiter Costs *** -</u>	<u>$ 20,000</u>
Total Cost Savings	$110,000/year

* Costs associated with administrative personnel that screen resumes and set up interviews. In an active recruiting program,

there is no need to screen hundreds of resumes that come in from newspaper advertisements because the recruiter will already have identified candidates for each open position in a more effective manner.

** Costs associated with a job remaining open for a month or longer while waiting for a qualified candidate to send in a resume. With active recruiting, the time that a position is open will be greatly reduced.

*** Fees paid to a recruiting agency to find candidates for open positions.

Step 3:   Assigning Resources

Once you have determined your current personnel inventory, present and future hiring needs, and justified your costs, you are ready to begin assigning resources to the process. The important consideration is the type of person that you assign as the recruiter. One option is to hire a recruiter from a recruiting agency, but this is not a necessity. The top recruiters in an agency can earn over $100,000 per year in commission and this can be an expensive option. Another option is to find someone with sales experience who understands how to build a network of contacts and does not mind extensive time on the phone. The necessary skills that you need to look for are:

- Ability to find and follow-up on leads.
- Organization.

- Good phone etiquette.
- Outgoing personality and talkative.
- Self-motivated and strong work ethic.

The ideal candidate would be someone from a telemarketing or telesales firm that has two or more years of experience of cold calling on potential customers. These candidates are less expensive than hiring an experienced recruiter and can easily adapt to an active recruiting process.

The office space that is used for recruiting activities is another important consideration. The space needs to be isolated from other office areas due to the amount of noise that will be generated. Recruiters will spend most of their day talking on the phone to potential candidates. It would be disruptive to mix the recruiters with other personnel that may be quietly focusing on their work.

The tools necessary for the recruiter are a computer, desk, telephone (preferably with a direct extension number and voice mail), access to the internet and e-mail, and a file cabinet. Another option is to develop a highly sophisticated computer database to store resumes and contact information.

Step 4:   Creating a Database of Potential Candidates

The most important part of any active recruiting process is the database of potential candidates. This is the network that is used to draw your future employees. The larger the database, the larger the pool of potential candidates. As mentioned earlier, this database can be a computerized system that stores all necessary information or it can be a very organized file cabinet. If you decide to use a computerized system, you will need to have it developed, which can take months and cost thousands of dollars. My belief is a good file cabinet that is properly organized is a better option. It is cheap and you do not have to wait for months to start using it. Electronic resumes can be stored on any Microsoft® Windows® based computer by using the Windows® Explorer File Manager program. This program will allow keyword searches of the resumes to find resumes with certain qualifications.

After determining how you want to store your information, the first step is to begin making contacts to build the database. Good sources to get started are current employees, old resumes and job applications, and the internet. Internet recruiting will be discussed later, so we will focus on other areas. Engage your recruiter to talk to current employees and get five names of friends or former colleagues who would make good employees. The next step would be to have them go through old resumes and job applications and get the name and phone number. Have them focus on areas where you will have hiring needs in the next six months. Once the recruiter has a few hundred names and phone numbers, he or she can begin calling the names on the list. In the next chapter, a more detailed explanation of phone calling potential candidates will be discussed. During the implementation phase, you will need to determine how you want to create your database and what method you want to use to store information.

Step 5: Creating Measurements and Standards

As with any business process, it is important to measure certain attributes and create standards that you want achieved. Measurements will allow you to monitor the process, maximize resources, and make sure that goals are met. The key measurements and standards of the recruiting process are described below.

Recruiting Phone Calls—This is a measure of how many phone calls the recruiter makes to candidates. A call is defined as actually talking to the candidate and gathering some information. Leaving a message for the candidate on their voice mail does not count as a call. If e-mail is the preferred method of communication with the candidate, then a call is defined as sending an e-mail requesting information and receiving a reply from the candidate. This measurement should be monitored on a daily basis. A competent recruiter should be able to complete 15 to 20 recruiting calls per day.

Recruiting Applicants—This is a measure of how many qualified candidates show interest in employment with your company and send you a resume. To count as a qualified applicant, the recruiter must do a short interview on the phone to determine salary information, skills, job experience, communication skills, and contact information. The standard number of recruiting applicants that can be gathered in a day will vary by profession, but over time you will be able to determine standards that reflect your process.

Interviews—This is the measure of the number of face-to-face interviews of candidates by managers in your company. Recruiter interviews are not counted in this measurement.

New hires—The number of new people hired using your process. This is the final output of your recruiting process.

Calls to Applicant Ratio—This is the ratio of the number of recruiting phone calls that must be made to get a recruiting applicant. It is calculated by dividing the total number of calls by the total number of applicants.

Applicant to Interview Ratio—This is the ratio of the number of applicants that it takes to find one who is qualified enough to be interviewed by the hiring manager. It is calculated by dividing the total number of applicants by the total number of interviews.

Interview to New Hire Ratio—This is the ratio of the number of candidates who must be interviewed to find one who is actually hired. It is calculated by dividing the total number of candidates interviewed by the total number of people hired.

The ratios described above are very important for planning purposes. For example, if you need to hire 20 employees over the next year, you can calculate how many phone calls it will take, how many people that you need to recruit, and how many interviews you will have to fulfill to hire 20 people. This will allow you to allocate your recruiting resources and monitor the progress of your recruiting process. It will take about three to six months of collecting statistics to get realistic ratios that can be used for planning. In the long run, you will be amazed at how accurate the numbers turn out. The active recruiting process is truly a numbers game. The more phone calls that are made, the more candidates that you will acquire and the more successful you will be at hiring qualified people.

Step 6: You Are Done and Ready to Start Recruiting

Now that you have identified your present personnel inventory, justified implementing the new recruiting process, assigned the proper recruiting resources, created the candidate database, and created measurements to monitor the process, you are ready to start recruiting. Always keep in mind that this is a long-term process and do not expect to get immediate results. Most projects of this type fail due to unrealistic expectations. Expect three to six months to build your database to a level that will produce results. Stay the course and see the project through to finality. You will not be disappointed. Many of the top recruiters have built up thousands of contacts through years of building their network. After a year of utilizing this recruiting process, you will reap huge rewards with many qualified candidates for each job opening.

Chapter 4

DAILY OPERATIONS AND FUNCTIONS OF THE ACTIVE RECRUITING PROCESS

Now that your recruiting process is in place, it is time to get down to business and begin actively recruiting candidates for your business. As mentioned in the previous chapter, the key components of your process are the recruiter and the database of potential candidates. To start building your database, a passive and active recruiting approach should be used.

The internet is a wonderful tool to advertise to potential candidates. It is much less expensive than newspaper advertisement and reaches more people. Using a job posting service on the internet will allow you to post numerous jobs for a monthly fee. You will need to investigate which job posting service best fits your company's needs.

In addition to internet postings, the recruiter will need to begin making outgoing calls to potential candidates to begin developing contacts. In the beginning, good sources of contacts are employees in the company, past job applicants, and searching the internet.

Using the Internet

A very aggressive strategy can be utilized by using the internet as a recruiting source. Beware of the dangers of relying solely on the internet as a source. Many companies fall into a trap of posting jobs on the internet and not using other sources to find candidates. Remember that the internet is not much different than an electronic newspaper advertisement and can have many shortcomings. Internet postings rely on a potential applicant viewing your job posting and contacting you to submit a resume. Using internet job postings is a passive approach that should supplement your active recruiting strategy, not replace it.

Selecting a job posting service is the most important part of the internet recruiting strategy. You should use a set of criteria to judge different services. Some items to consider are:

Costs: Internet job posting services vary in costs from a few hundred dollars per year to several thousand. Set constraints on how much you want to spend.

Niche: Many services cater to a niche in the job market such as technical or administrative. You will need to determine if you need to cater to a certain job market or want to cover all job markets.

Geographic Area: Although the internet can be viewed worldwide, many services cater to a particular geographic area. If your strategy is to recruit only from a particular area, you may want to consider one of these services.

Exposure: Some of the larger job posting boards advertise a considerable amount to drive traffic to their job site. You will need to consider the exposure that your company's job postings will get. It is not beneficial to post jobs on the internet if no one sees them.

Resume Databases: Many of the larger services have resume databases that can be accessed by employers. This is a good source of potential candidates that can help you build your candidate database.

Once you have selected a job posting service that fits your needs, it is important to start posting jobs immediately. Do not just post jobs where you have an immediate opening, but post jobs where you may have a need over the next six months. You will need to have a flow of applicants before you actually have an opening. Waiting until a job becomes available will severely limit the effectiveness of your recruiting process.

Writing an Effective Job Posting: The most important part of using a job posting service is writing a job posting that captures the attention of the potential candidate. You must have a writing style that sells your job opportunity and your company. The posting should include a job description as well as an explanation of the benefits to the potential candidate. Here is an example of an effective posting.

> "HOT!! Visual Basic Programming Opportunity
> Our company is a cutting edge software development business and a leader in the web development

market. We are seeking a hotshot Visual Basic programmer with at least 3 years of development experience to join our development team. You will be working with the latest software technology with an established company. Our salaries and benefits are among the best in the industry and our employees receive continuing education to keep you updated with the latest technology. If you are interested in developing the future of internet technology, please contact us."

Keep your postings short and to the point. Too much information can discourage some potential candidates from applying. The goal of your posting should be to get as many possible candidates to apply. This will build your total number of contacts in your database and give you a larger pool of potential candidates for future openings.

<u>Other Internet Search Techniques</u>: Many people have personal websites where they post their resumes. There are some effective methods of searching the internet to find these resumes. Search engines are available where you can provide search criteria to the engine to search available websites. You can experiment with different search criteria to find a multitude of potential candidates.

Other Sources of Contacts

As mentioned earlier, the goal of your recruiting process is to build a network of potential candidates. There are many good sources to help you find out where to find candidates.

<u>Current Employees</u>: Have the recruiter talk to the current employees within the company. The recruiter's goal should be to get at least five names and phone numbers from each employee. Former colleagues, managers, and friends are all good contacts.

<u>Former Applicants</u>: The recruiter should review past job applications of people that have applied for employment with your company. Even if the person was not qualified at the time of the application, they may have gained more experience or received a college degree since they applied for employment.

<u>Clubs, Associations, and User Groups</u>: Find local organizations that cater to people with certain skills that are used by your company. For example, if your company has a large engineering department, there are professional associations that cater to different engineering professions. Many of these organizations will work with employers to help their members find new employment. It may be beneficial to attend the organization's monthly meeting to promote your company and the opportunities that are available.

<u>State Databases of Licensed Professionals</u>: Many professionals such as nurses, doctors, pharmacists, architects, and lawyers are required to be licensed in the state in which they

work. These databases may be obtained from the state licensing board. If you are recruiting licensed professionals, these databases will give you a wealth of contacts for your networking efforts.

Get on the Phone

The telephone is the recruiter's best friend. It is the connection between your business and the candidates. Your recruiter has now acquired many contacts, but the process does not move forward until these people are contacted. Each workday should have at least two hours dedicated to contacting people on the phone. Many people work during the day, so the best time to call may be after hours when people are at home. If you have an e-mail address or cell phone number of your contacts, then you can contact them anytime. Avoid contacting potential candidates on their work phone or work e-mail. This can be viewed as unethical or even illegal in some areas.

Organization and planning are important to make effective calls and maximize the time on the phone. Each day, the recruiter needs to make a plan of who he or she is going to call, how many calls are going to made, and which call scripts are going to be used. The recruiters must also decide what they want to accomplish from their calls.

The goal of each phone call is to gather information about the candidate. Notes should be taken on each call regarding the candidate's qualifications, job history, salary history, contact information, and career goals. During the phone call, the recruiter should try to get referrals of other potential candidates. A simple form can be used to take notes during the call to capture vital information. This form along with a resume or other information can be kept in a file folder for future reference. Form 4-1 illustrates a typical candidate information form.

Form 4-1: Candidate Information Form	
Name: Contact Information Home: Cell: E-mail:	Address:
Skills: (skill, years of experience)	
Education:	
Salary Information Current Salary: Desired Salary:	
Career Goals: (type of company, type of job, industry)	
Referrals:	
Other Information:	

In addition to the candidate information form, there are other tools to help the recruiter make effective calls.

<u>Call Scripts:</u> When making cold calls to potential candidates, an effective call script can keep a candidate's attention and while getting important information. An indirect approach is many times more effective than a direct approach. Some examples of indirect scripts that lead into the conversation are:

> "Hi, my name is Steve and I work for XYZ Corporation. The reason I am calling you is I am try-ing to locate some top-notch computer programmers and I thought that you may be able to help me out. You were referred to me by some employees in our office who thought you might know of some pro-grammers that are in the job market."

> "Hi, my name is Steve and I work for XYZ Corporation. The reason I am calling you is that I am networking with computer programmers in this area and I thought you may be able to help me out. Based on what I have heard from other programmers in the area, you have a great reputation in the indus-try and might know of some people that are inter-ested in new career opportunities."

With an indirect approach, begin the conversation by asking for referrals then lead into a direct conversation about the can-didate's own career goals and skills. This approach will not only tell you about the candidate, but help get referrals. Every phone call should ask the candidate "who do you know that may fit our requirements?" Always give your name, business name, and phone number to the candidate to generate future referrals.

A direct approach can be used for candidates that send you a resume in response to a job posting or if you are calling a former job applicant. An example of a direct approach script:

> "Hi, this is Steve from XYZ Corporation. You sent a resume to our company a while back and I have some questions about your background."

Each recruiter should try different approaches until he or she develops a style that works best for them.

Call List: A tool used by the recruiter to organize calls is a call list. The call list arranges the daily calls in an easy to use form that makes it easy to go from one call to another. Form 4-2 illustrates a typical call list used by recruiting agencies.

Form 4-2: Recruiter Call List

Recruiter:		Date:
Candidate Name	Phone Number	Results of Call

Obtain a Resume

If possible, have the potential candidate e-mail a resume. The resume should be sent as an attachment to the e-mail and should be in a word processing or text format. Once the resume is received, it should be kept in a file folder on the recruiter's computer with all other resumes. Computer file folders containing resumes can be organized by department or skill-set to keep similar resumes together.

If the computer has a Microsoft® Windows® operating system, the Windows® Explorer File Manager program can be used to query the resume files by keyword. To use this function, click on the Start button on the Windows® toolbar, then click on Programs and Windows® Explorer. The Windows® Explorer program will open and show all file folders on the computer. Once in the Windows® Explorer program, click on "File" in the toolbar, then "New", then "Folder". An icon of the folder will show up and you can edit the name of the folder. Rename the folder "Resumes". You can then save all of the resumes that are received in this folder.

To search for resumes by keyword, click on "Tools" in the Windows® Explorer toolbar, then click "Find", then click "Files or Folders". The "Find: All Files" dialogue box will appear. In the "Containing text" field, type in the search criteria that you are seeking (i.e. mechanical engineer). Then in the "Look In" field, choose the "Resumes" folder. Finally, click the "Find Files" button. Windows® Explorer will search all files in the "Resumes" folder containing the text you are seeking.

This feature will allow the recruiter to find all resumes that contain a certain skill-set, location, or industry. When a job opening becomes available, the recruiter can easily retrieve all of the resumes that contain the skills required for the job.

Follow Up

Once initial contact is made with the potential candidate and information is gathered, it is extremely important to follow up on a regular basis. Part of the recruiter's job is not only seeking out new candidates, but building relationships with existing candidates. Over time, the structure of the recruiter's calls will shift from 100% cold calling to about 50% cold calling and 50% follow up calling. Potential candidates relocate, change jobs, gain skills, and increase their experience level, so it is necessary to maintain contact with them at least once a year. Following up with candidates will also produce numerous referrals from the candidates.

When the company has an immediate need to hire someone, all qualified candidates in the database need to be contacted. If the data is not updated on a regular basis, it may be impossible to locate the candidates.

A "tickler" file system should be set up that gives the recruiter a system of following up with a candidate on a regular basis. This system will keep files organized and insures that each candidate is contacted on a predetermined schedule. Areas of your business where there is a high risk of losing employees or

where there is potential future growth, will need special attention. Potential candidates that fit a need in these areas will
need to be contacted more often.

Another tool that can be used to aide the recruiter is a computerized calendar or task scheduler. Many businesses use
Microsoft® Outlook for e-mail, but it also contains a very
good task scheduler. The recruiter can set-up a schedule to call
potential candidates and Outlook will remind the recruiter
when the task must be completed. There are other task sched-
uling software packages available and all are adequate to meet
the needs of the recruiter.

Chapter 5

THE INTERVIEWING AND HIRING PROCESS

When a job opening becomes available, the process of interviewing and hiring can begin. If the active recruiting process has been followed, a number of qualified candidates should be identified and contacted. The recruiter should have some information regarding the candidate's skill level, salary requirements, and career goals. This information will allow the recruiter to narrow the number of candidates down to the best-qualified people.

These candidates should be contacted on the phone and the recruiter should perform a short phone interview to verify all pertinent information, collect references, and schedule a face-to-face interview with the hiring manager.

The Interviewing Process

A short but thorough interviewing process should be followed. Because of the shortage of qualified candidates, many candidates may have multiple job opportunities. The company that moves quickly will be more likely to hire a highly sought after candidate.

A one-step interviewing approach should be utilized. Schedule the candidate into the office to meet with all managers who are involved in the decision making process. If the candidate is required to take a test to measure skills, the test should be administered during the interview. It is important to complete all interviewing and testing duties in one step. Many candidates are gainfully employed and may have trouble getting away from their present employer to interview. Multiple steps in the process can discourage a prospective candidate and cause your company to miss out on a good candidate.

During the interviewing process, someone from the human resources department should meet with the candidate to discuss the candidate's salary requirements, the company benefits, and company policies. This information is important to the candidate's decision-making process. As the candidate leaves the interview, he or she should have a good idea of the work environment, job requirements, and company benefits.

Once the first step is completed, the hiring managers should meet and make a decision to approve or reject the candidate. If the decision is to approve the candidate, the recruiter needs to check the references of the candidate, verify college degrees, and verify employment history. To check references, a standard questionnaire should be used that verifies the candidate's skill level and explores the candidate's ability to work with others. The references should be called and asked the questions from the questionnaire. Form 5-1 illustrates a typical form that can be used.

Form 5-1: Reference Check Form

Candidate's Name:
Reference Name:
Type of Reference (Supervisor, Peer, Other):
Date:

How long and in what capacity did you know _____?

What did _____ do for you?

On a scale of 1 to 5 (5 being the best rating), please rate his or her job performance:

Quality of Work:
Reliability:
Ability to work with co-workers:
Ability to work with supervisors:
Work Ethic:

What are some of his or her weaknesses?

What are some of his or her strengths?

If given the opportunity, would _____ be eligible to rehire?

Additional comments?

This form, once completed, can be sent to each hiring manager via e-mail to aide their decision making process. College degrees can be easily verified by contacting the registrar's office of the college. The candidate's social security number is necessary for verification.

Urgency and speed are important. The interview process should be streamlined so that qualified candidates are not lost to other interested employers. The total time involved in interviewing, testing, checking references, and making a decision should be less than five working days.

Making the Job Offer

Once the interviewing process is completed and the hiring decision is made, it is time to make the job offer to the candidate. Just as in the selling process, the recruiting process must be able to close the sell to the candidate. Based on prior discussions by the recruiter and human resources personnel with the candidate, there should be a good understanding of the type of job offer that the candidate is seeking. If the offer does not meet the candidate's requirements, it will most likely be rejected.

A company representative should call the candidate and make the offer over the phone. This conversation will give the company representative a good idea if the offer is acceptable to the candidate. Once the offer is made over the phone, a job offer letter should be drafted and sent to the candidate. A short time frame should be given for the candidate to make a decision. A follow up phone call should be made two or three days after the offer letter is sent to verify that the letter was received. During this call, the company representative should ask the candidate if he or she is ready to accept the offer.

The biggest mistake that businesses make during the offer stage is giving the candidate too much time to make a decision. Believe it or not, many candidates will take a job offer to other employers to try to get a better deal. This is called "offer shopping". To avoid "offer shopping", the candidate should be required to make a decision within two or three days of receiving the offer letter.

If the recruiting and interviewing process is correctly followed, the company should feel confident that the offer will be accepted.

Have a Backup Plan

When the offer stage is reached in the hiring process, it is vital to have a backup plan. Do not put all of your efforts into one candidate. If the candidate decides not to accept the offer, the process can be set back for days or even weeks. While making the offer to one candidate, have other candidates ready to interview. If the offer is rejected, you will be ready with replacements.

The backup candidates will also provide leverage to help you close the prime candidate. Let the prime candidate know that there are other people that you are considering for the position and he or she needs to make a decision on the offer.

This will create a sense of urgency and move the process forward. Remember, your number one concern is filling the position as quickly as possible to avoid productivity losses by your company.

Reviewing the Entire Recruiting, Interviewing, and Hiring Process

Now that all of the pieces of the recruiting puzzle have been discussed, it is time to review the entire process. Figure 5-2 shows a diagram of the process from start to finish.

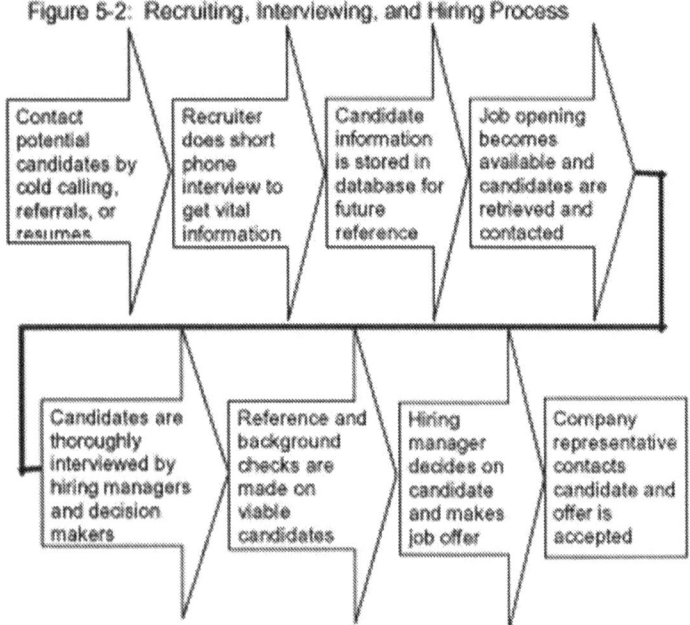

Figure 5-2: Recruiting, Interviewing, and Hiring Process

Following an active recruiting approach will allow your company to find, interview, and hire those candidates who you missed in the past. If properly followed, the recruiting and hiring process will be much more efficient and the overall productivity of your company's workforce will increase. Your company will have an advantage over the competition because you will be able to find better candidates, hire them quickly, and begin reaping the benefits much faster. The company that can move quickly will be successful into the twenty first century.

Chapter 6

USING THE ACTIVE RECRUITING PROCESS TO RETAIN EMPLOYEES AND DEVELOP NEW REVENUE STREAMS

Once the active recruiting process is implemented, there are many other benefits that will be realized. Your company will have a wealth of new information that has value. Salary data, names, addresses, phone numbers are all valuable data that has many uses.

Salary Information

Businesses spend thousands of dollars each year to make sure they are paying competitive salaries. Most employees leave their employers because they can get a better salary with another company. Paying your employees competitive salaries will allow you to retain your best employees.

Most companies purchase salary survey information from outside sources, which can be very expensive. The problem with these surveys is they are not very accurate and the information can be outdated. The database of potential candidates that is created through the active recruiting process will contain salary information of these candidates. This information can be summarized by skill-set, giving you a real time, updated source of salary information. Analysis of this salary information will tell you the market value of your present employees. You will be able to adjust your company's salary structure to remain competitive in the marketplace.

When budgeting for a new project, you will be able to estimate labor costs based on the information in the database. By having accurate salary information, a better estimate of return on investment for the project can be achieved and better business decisions can be made.

Salary information can provide your company with additional revenue streams by selling this information to other businesses. Instead of buying salary surveys from another source, you will be able to sell the information on the market and increase revenue to your company.

Marketing Information

If your business markets its products to individual consumers, your recruiting database will have thousands of contacts that can be used to market your company's products. The database will contain valuable information, such as household income and the candidate's interests, for your marketing efforts. This information can be used for marketing mailers or telemarketing efforts. You will have the ability to reach more potential consumers and target certain market segments.

Another benefit is a continued exposure of your company to these potential candidates. When the recruiter contacts the candidates, they will recognize the company name and have a more positive image of your company. This name recognition is a great recruiting tool and will also increase revenue to your company.

Many companies spend thousands of dollars to obtain mailing lists or consumer lists to market their products. The recruiting database can supplement these lists to further expand exposure of your company's products to more consumers.

REVIEW AND CLOSING

The job market over the next decade will provide substantial challenges to businesses. It will be difficult to find, hire, and retain employees due to the increased competition for a smaller pool of potential employees. The businesses that can actively recruit these candidates will have a huge advantage. Following the active recruiting process outlined in this book will give you a world-class recruiting program.

Apply a winning sales attitude to recruiting and make every effort to reach every candidate in your market. Using this method, your business will find candidates that you never reached before. Remember, determination and consistent effort are the keys to success.

In the long run, your business will realize enormous benefits such as improved productivity and decreased costs. New projects and product launches will be implemented with extraordinary speed. Businesses that can bring their products to market quicker will be on the leading edge, instead of following the competition.

You will now have the tools to move your business forward by recruiting and retaining a quality workforce. Follow this step-by-step approach, stick to the program, and you will develop a valuable process that can be used for years to come.

Changing how you do business is always a difficult course of action, but the benefits far outweigh the hardships. Change is prevalent in business today. Companies that improve their processes will remain ahead of the curve and will lead the competition. By taking a proactive approach, your business will be at the forefront.

Do not wait to get started. Steps can be taken immediately to begin implementing the active recruiting process. The sooner you start, the sooner you can begin reaping the benefits. Now go out there and begin building your own world-class recruiting process.

ABOUT THE AUTHOR

Steve Bullard has been helping businesses with their staffing problems for seven years. His clients have ranged from Fortune 500 companies to pre-IPO start-up businesses. His solutions have given his clients the tools necessary to recruit top-level employees.

Bullard holds a Bachelor of Science in Industrial Engineering from Texas A&M University. After graduation, he went to work for Clarke American Incorporated in San Antonio, Texas as a Process Engineer. His duties included redesigning business and sales processes to improve efficiency and reduce cycle times. In addition to process engineering, he also taught Total Quality Management classes and helped implement TQM philosophies at Clarke American. He worked on many large-scale projects that included implementing new manufacturing technology and sales force automation.

After six years of service to Clarke American, Bullard decided to change careers and joined Data Staffing Centre in Houston, Texas as a Technical Recruiter. He quickly became a successful recruiter and built an impressive list of clients. After two years with Data Staffing Centre, he left to start his own recruiting business. By providing unique staffing solutions to his clients,

Bullard was able to distinguish himself from other recruiting agencies.

He currently uses his experience as a top recruiter to advise businesses on implementing world-class recruiting processes. He continues to run his consulting business in Houston, Texas and participates in numerous speaking engagements.

Notes

You may have some great ideas for your own business. Use this space to write down any ideas that you have.

Notes

Notes

Notes

Notes

Notes

Notes

Notes

Notes

Notes

Notes

Notes

Notes

Notes

Notes

Notes

Notes

Notes

Notes

Notes

Notes

Notes

Notes

Notes

Notes

Notes

Notes

Notes

Notes

Notes

Notes

Notes

Notes

Notes

Notes

Notes

Notes

Notes

Notes

INDEX

Active recruiting, 10-15, 17-20, 24-26, 39, 45, 47-48, 51-52

Backup plan, 43

Call list, 34

Call scripts

    Indirect approach, 33

    Direct approach, 33-34

Candidate database, 24, 27

Candidate Information Form, 31, 33

Cold calling, 7, 20, 37

Contact sources

    Current employees, 21, 29

    Former applicants, 29

    Clubs and associations, 29

Cost justification

    Incremental cost, 17

    Cost savings, 18

Effective calls, 30, 33

Follow up calls, 43

Growth areas, 16

Job offer, 42-43

Marketing information, 48

Microsoft® tools

    Outlook, 38

    Calendar, 38

    Windows® Explorer, 21, 36

Office space requirements, 20

Passive recruiting, 10, 12

Personnel inventory, 15-16, 19, 24

Population shift, 2

Process map, 15

Recruiter tools, 33-34

Recruiting measurements

    Phone calls, 7, 14, 22-24

    Applicants, 22-23, 25, 27, 29

    Interviews, 18, 23-24

    New hires, 17, 23

    Calls to Applicant Ratio, 23

    Applicant to Interview Ratio, 23

    Interview to Hire Ratio, 23

Reference Check Form, 41

References, 39-40, 42

Risk areas, 16

Salary information, 22, 47-48

Sales Model, 5-7

Tickler file, 37

Using the internet

    Job posting service, 18, 25-27

    Writing a job posting, 27

    Internet searches, 28

Workforce demographics, 1

Workforce education, 3

0-595-26362-3